Wars Waged Under the Microscope

The War Against Ebola

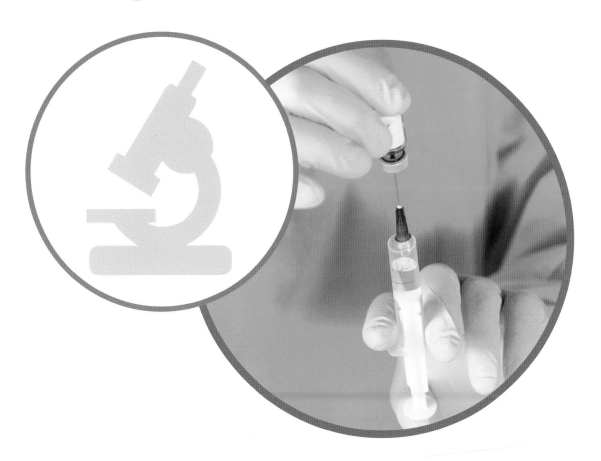

Sarah Eason

CRABTREE
PUBLISHING COMPANY
WWW.CRABTREEBOOKS.COM

CRABTREE
PUBLISHING COMPANY
WWW.CRABTREEBOOKS.COM

Author: Sarah Eason

Editors: Jennifer Sanderson and Ellen Rodger

Editorial director: Kathy Middleton

Design: Simon Borrough

Cover design and additional artwork:
 Katherine Berti

Photo research: Rachel Blount

Proofreader: Wendy Scavuzzo

**Production coordinator and
 Prepress technician:** Ken Wright

Print coordinator: Katherine Berti

Consultant: David Hawksett

Produced for Crabtree Publishing by Calcium Creative Ltd

Photo Credits

Cover: tr: National Institute of Allergy and Infectious Diseases (NIAID), Wikimedia Commons; All other images Shutterstock

Inside: Centers for Disease Control and Prevention: Brian Bird, Ph.D. D.V.M., Veterinary Medical Officer, Viral Special Pathogens Branch/CDC Connects: p. 23; Amy Schuh, PhD, MPH: p. 16; Heidi Soeters, PhD, MPH: pp. 21, 27; Flickr: CDC Global: p. 9; Shutterstock: p. 4, Anton Ivanov: p. 10; Anyaivanova: p. 15; Avatar_023: p. 24; Leonie Broekstra: p. 6; Chaikom: p. 13; Elizaveta Galitckaia: p. 11; La Zona: p. 5; Riccardo Mayer: p. 18; Belen B Massieu: p. 8; Micolas: p. 26; Yaw Niel: p. 22; Nixx Photography: p. 14; Peterschreiber.media: p. 25; SciePro: pp. 12, 28; Rattiya Thongdumhyu: pp. 17, 29; Vandathai: p. 7; Sarit Wuttisan: p. 19; Wikimedia Commons: Athalia Christie/CDC Global: p. 20.

Library and Archives Canada Cataloguing in Publication

Title: The war against Ebola / Sarah Eason.
Names: Eason, Sarah, author.
Description: Series statement: Wars waged under the microscope
 | Includes bibliographical references and index.
Identifiers: Canadiana (print) 20210189118 |
 Canadiana (ebook) 20210189126 |
 ISBN 9781427151292 (hardcover) |
 ISBN 9781427151377 (softcover) |
 ISBN 9781427151452 (HTML) |
 ISBN 9781427151537 (EPUB)
Subjects: LCSH: Ebola virus disease—Juvenile literature. |
 LCSH: Ebola virus disease—Treatment—Juvenile literature. |
 LCSH: Ebola virus disease—Prevention—Juvenile literature. |
 LCSH: Epidemics—Juvenile literature.
Classification: LCC RC140.5 .E25 2022 | DDC j614.5/88—dc23

Library of Congress Cataloging-in-Publication Data

Names: Eason, Sarah, author.
Title: The war against Ebola / Sarah Eason.
Description: New York, NY : Crabtree Publishing Company,
 [2022] | Series: Wars waged under the microscope |
 Includes index.
Identifiers: LCCN 2021016652 (print) |
 LCCN 2021016653 (ebook) |
 ISBN 9781427151292 (hardcover) |
 ISBN 9781427151377 (paperback) |
 ISBN 9781427151452 (ebook) |
 ISBN 9781427151537 (epub)
Subjects: LCSH: Ebola virus disease--Juvenile literature. |
 Ebola virus disease--Treatment--Juvenile literature. |
 Ebola virus disease--Prevention--Juvenile literature. |
 Epidemics--Juvenile literature.
Classification: LCC RC140.5 .E25 2022 (print) |
 LCC RC140.5 (ebook) | DDC 614.5/88--dc23
LC record available at https://lccn.loc.gov/2021016652
LC ebook record available at https://lccn.loc.gov/2021016653

Crabtree Publishing Company
www.crabtreebooks.com   1-800-387-7650

Printed in the U.S.A./062021/CG20210401

Published in Canada
Crabtree Publishing
616 Welland Ave.
St. Catharines, Ontario
L2M 5V6

Published in the United States
Crabtree Publishing
347 Fifth Ave.
Suite 1402-145
New York, NY 10016

Contents

The Enemy

Ebola is a rare and deadly disease that is caused by a **virus**. A virus is an extremely tiny **organism** that is too small to be seen by the unaided human eye. Ebola is most often found in bats and in **primates**—such as chimpanzees, gorillas, monkeys, and humans. The first case of Ebola occurred in 1976 in Africa, and that is where **outbreaks** of the disease have mainly taken place ever since.

The Ebola virus is one of a number of viruses that are known to pass between animal species. The virus is found inside fruit bats, like this one.

A Super Spreader

Many scientists believe that the first outbreak of Ebola in humans was caused by a person coming into contact with an animal, such as a monkey, that had the disease. Once the virus was inside that person, it quickly spread to other people. The Ebola virus is highly contagious, which means it spreads easily from person to person. Since the first outbreak of Ebola in 1976, there have been thousands of deaths in Africa because of the disease.

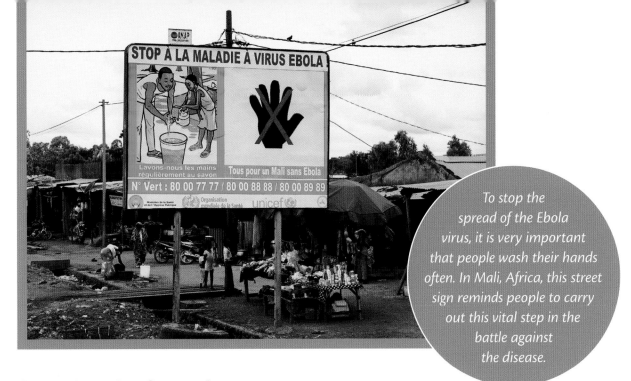

To stop the spread of the Ebola virus, it is very important that people wash their hands often. In Mali, Africa, this street sign reminds people to carry out this vital step in the battle against the disease.

Stopping the Spread

Although Ebola has mainly affected countries in Africa, small outbreaks of the disease have taken place in other places, too. These include Russia, the United States, the United Kingdom (UK), Italy, and Spain. However, because scientists quickly became aware how dangerous the disease was, they were able to contain it and the virus did not spread widely in non-African countries. Although there is currently no cure for Ebola, scientists around the world are working hard to find one so they can defeat this deadly killer.

"The world knows how to fight this disease. It's not a mystery. We know the science. We know how to prevent it from spreading. We know how to care for those who contract it. We know that if we take the proper steps, we can save lives. But we have to act fast."

Barack Obama, President of the United States 2009—2017

The Battle Begins

Ebola was first discovered in 1976 near the Ebola River in West Africa. In the summer, a small hospital in Zaire (now known as the Democratic Republic of the Congo, or DRC), started seeing patients that had bleeding from the eyes, ears, and nose; stomach pains; headaches; and fever. At first, the hospital staff thought it was **malaria** or another infection they knew. Soon they realized it was a disease like no other they had come across before.

A Mystery Enemy

In the hospital, nearly all the patients who had the mysterious sickness died, and more and more people were getting sick. Eventually, a doctor sent a blood **sample** from one of the sick patients to the Institute of Tropical Medicine (ITM) in Belgium in Europe. There, they discovered the cause of the illness was a new virus. A team of scientists from Belgium flew to Zaire. The team's first job was to find out how the virus was spreading.

When researchers in Belgium received blood samples from sick patients in Zaire, they realized they were dealing with a brand-new and highly dangerous disease.

Tracking the Enemy

By visiting the villages surrounding the hospital in Zaire, the scientists discovered that many of those infected with the new virus had been to the hospital recently. Many had had an injection of some kind with needles that were reused from one patient to another, with up to 600 patients per day being treated with reused needles.

Scientists also realized that a lot of people were becoming infected after burying those who had died from the illness. This led the experts to the understanding that the disease was being passed from person to person through touch and bodily fluids such as saliva and tears. Educating people—including health care workers—about this deadly spread was to be the first step in the battle against Ebola.

*Today, hospital staff are trained to carefully **dispose** of used needles. However, reusing needles **contaminated** with Ebola virus likely caused the speedy **transmission** of the disease in Zaire in 1976.*

"Protection of healthcare workers is important for two reasons... number one, so they don't get infected and take it home to their families; and number two... so healthcare workers don't just carry the infection from one patient to another."

David Heymann, professor at the London School of Hygiene and Tropical Medicine

Knowing the Enemy

The African countries where Ebola outbreaks have occurred are often poor and do not have the resources needed to treat the illness and to keep people safe. These resources include medical equipment, but also all-important education.

Specialist teams must remove the bodies of people who have died of Ebola to prevent transmission.

A Place to Die

One of the biggest problems in tackling early outbreaks of Ebola in Africa was that many people were **suspicious** of the hospitals where people were being treated for the disease. People felt that hospitals were dangerous places where patients went to die, and they did not trust the staff there. As a result, when people became sick with Ebola, rather than going to the hospital, they stayed at home and were cared for by their families. Unfortunately, this led to even more transmissions of the disease. Teaching people to trust the staff in hospitals has been very important in the fight against Ebola.

CASE STUDY: EDUCATING PEOPLE

In 2014, an Ebola outbreak began in Sierra Leone in Africa. To help educate local people about the disease, Médecins Sans Frontières and the **World Health Organization (WHO)** sent experts to the country to explain how Ebola spreads. They also trained more than 300 **volunteers** to track down, trace, and record suspected cases of Ebola.

The volunteers went into **remote** villages and gave people advice on how to control the spread of the disease by not hugging and touching, and by frequent handwashing. One of the most important issues they had to explain was how to safely bury the bodies of people who had died of Ebola.

Scientists had discovered that the Ebola virus lived on a body for days after the person had died, and so could spread to others even after death. In parts of Africa, family members prepare a body for burial by washing and dressing it. If the person had Ebola, this was very dangerous. People were forced to bury their dead without the rituals, which was very distressing for them.

Volunteers visited villagers to help explain the symptoms, or signs, of Ebola and how important it is for anyone who feels sick to seek medical help immediately.

An Invisible Threat

Like all viruses, the Ebola virus is a microorganism, or microbe. Microorganisms are small living things that can only be seen with a **microscope**. They are all around us—in the soil, air, and water. Only some microbes, such as the Ebola virus, are harmful to people.

Virus Invasion

Like all viruses, Ebola can replicate, or make copies of itself, only inside the body of another living organism. The virus travels from one organism to another in bodily fluids, such as blood or saliva. Once inside a body, the virus invades the body's **cells**. There, it replicates. Those copies then spread to other cells, and the virus takes over.

People often touch their nose, eyes, and mouth. If their hands have been in contact with a virus, it is then easily passed into the body.

Catching the Invisible

People catch Ebola virus by coming into contact with the bodily fluids of another organism that has the virus. Bodily fluids include saliva, blood, tears, urine, vomit, and feces, or waste. For example, the relatives of a person sick with Ebola may care for the sick person by wiping away saliva or vomit when the person is sick. The virus is then on the caregivers hands. If the caregiver then touches their own eyes, nose, or mouth before handwashing, the virus enters their body, and the person becomes infected.

Deadly for Days

Ebola virus is an especially deadly virus because it can survive in bodily fluids outside of the body for several days. If these fluids are touched by another person, they can become infected. However, unlike some other types of viruses, such as the flu virus, Ebola cannot be transmitted by traveling through the air.

*Modern labs have **electron microscopes** for studying microorgansisms. These powerful microscopes use a beam of electrons to magnify objects, or make them bigger, so that they can be seen. This scientist is studying an image of **bacteria**, which was captured using an electron microscope.*

Under Attack

Our first line of defense against virus invasion is our **immune system**. The immune cells protect the body against attack from viruses and bacteria. When the immune cells detect an enemy—such as a virus—inside the body, they send **white blood cells** to destroy the invader.

White blood cells help the body keep healthy. If they are targeted by invaders, such as Ebola, the body becomes sick.

How the Virus Works

The problem with Ebola virus is that as soon as it gets inside a body, it quickly attacks the immune cells before they have a chance to send signals to the white blood cells. This allows the Ebola virus to then replicate and spread through the body.

As the virus travels through the bloodstream, it takes over cells and causes them to become coagulated. This means they form thick, solid lumps, which then stick to other cells, making even bigger lumps called clots. The lumpy clots then stick to and damage the lining of the **blood vessels**, causing bleeding inside the body. This is known as internal bleeding and is one of the symptoms of Ebola. Ebola can also lead to bleeding from different parts of the body, such as the eyes and nose.

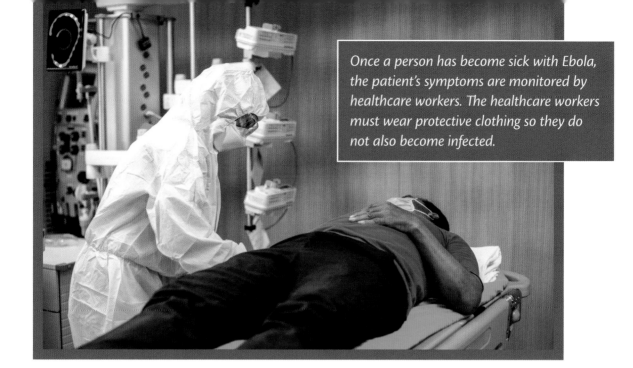

Once a person has become sick with Ebola, the patient's symptoms are monitored by healthcare workers. The healthcare workers must wear protective clothing so they do not also become infected.

The Enemy Becomes Stronger

Once a person is infected with a virus, it can be days or weeks before they show any symptoms. During that time, the virus is incubating, or growing and getting stronger. Some viruses can be passed on while they are still incubating. The Ebola virus is passed on only when the person shows symptoms. In addition to bleeding, these include fever, headaches, joint pain, stomachache, vomiting, tiredness, a rash, and red eyes.

UNDER THE MICROSCOPE

During an outbreak of Ebola in 2000, scientists studied many blood samples taken from Ebola patients to try to understand why some people die and other people become sick but survive. They discovered that survivors have a type of **gene** that signals the body to repair damaged blood vessels. There is still a long way to go but this could lead to new treatments for people who contract the disease.

Studying the Enemy

The Ebola virus is an unusual shape and is much bigger than other viruses, which are normally round and spiky. The only other virus like Ebola is the Marburg virus, which is passed from monkeys to humans.

The unusual shape of the Ebola virus can be seen here. The virus is long, rather than round and spiky like other viruses, and looks a little like a worm.

A Cell Invader

Virologists are scientists who study viruses. They have studied the Ebola virus in depth to discover how it operates once inside the human body. Once the virus enters a human, it attaches itself to a cell at a point called a receptor site, which acts a little like a docking site. Once there, the Ebola virus "ruffles up" the membrane, or outer lining of the cell, to make it easier to get into it. The virus then attaches its own membrane to the cell's membrane, and then slowly seeps inside.

Copy Me

Once inside the cell, the virus's next job is to "translate" all of the information about it, called its genetic code, into a language that the cell can recognize. It does this by releasing a substance called ribonucleic acid (RNA).

Tricking Cells

The RNA acts like a message to the cell, tricking it into thinking that the virus's genetic code is safe and fine to copy. The human cell then begins to copy the genetic code, and make many copies of the Ebola virus. These copies then break out of the cell, and spread throughout the body to other cells, where the process is repeated.

UNDER THE MICROSCOPE

Scientists are learning more about Ebola all the time, which gives them further clues about how to fight it. Fluorescence microscopy allows scientists to watch microscopic structures, such as cells infected with Ebola virus, by tagging them with inks. The ink allows researchers to look in detail at the cells. On viewing them, scientists have discovered that Ebola virus fills the cells with a protein called VP40. Filled to the bursting point, the cells bulge outward, causing small, needlelike points filled with VP40 to stick out. Scientists believe these little "needles" may then be able to prick and infect nearby cells, helping Ebola virus spread incredibly rapidly through the body.

By tagging microscopic structures with fluorescent ink, scientists can use a microscope to learn more about what they look like and how they behave.

The Importance of Testing

Once inside the body, Ebola spreads rapidly—then quickly passes to other people. To stop Ebola from spreading, it is very important to **diagnose** cases early. However, this can be difficult because early symptoms such as fever, headache, and weakness are very similar to other diseases, such as malaria and **typhoid fever**.

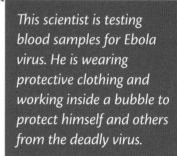

This scientist is testing blood samples for Ebola virus. He is wearing protective clothing and working inside a bubble to protect himself and others from the deadly virus.

Looking for the Signs

To test for Ebola virus, health care workers look for a mixture of symptoms that are usually seen in Ebola patients. At the same time, they confirm that the patient has come into contact with a source of Ebola virus within 21 days of their first symptoms. Blood samples are then taken from the patient for testing to confirm that they are infected with Ebola.

Testing for Ebola

To test if a person has Ebola, scientists can do a polymerase chain reaction (PCR) test. This test can detect even just a few particles, or bits, of the Ebola virus in a blood sample. These are present when the virus has only recently entered the body. This makes the test particularly useful in finding, **isolating**, and treating Ebola patients as quickly as possible.

CASE STUDY: LIFE-SAVING MACHINE

Testing has shown that one of the most important things when treating a patient with Ebola is to treat it quickly and efficiently before the virus can spread inside the body. In the DRC in June 2020, a patient suddenly died from **hemorrhagic fever**. The local health officials sent a specialist rapid response team to take samples and do tests to find out if it was Ebola. The next day, the laboratory confirmed that it was Ebola and safety measures were swiftly put in place to stop the disease from spreading.

The speed of this action was because of a plan set up by the WHO. In 2018, the WHO trained 25 **technicians** to use a machine called the GeneXpert. The GeneXpert can be set up in **rural** areas that have an outbreak to test samples quickly and safely. This allows health officials to act swiftly, tracking and tracing people who might be infected, isolating them, and controlling the spread of the disease.

The GeneXpert is used to test samples for Ebola using the PCR test. The results of the tests are available in hours, rather than days.

Armed with Medicine

Once someone is diagnosed with Ebola, treatment must be fast to give the patient the best chance of surviving.

Fighting Fluids

We know that Ebola attacks a person's immune system, and that the system needs to be properly **hydrated** to work well. Doctors treating patients with Ebola focus on keeping them well hydrated to help their immune system function properly.

It is doubly important to make sure patients are well hydrated because Ebola causes severe vomiting and diarrhea, which result in dehydration. Dehydration is when the body loses more fluid than it takes in. Patients are rehydrated to treat dehydration.

*To **rehydrate** the body, patients may be given oral rehydration therapy (ORT), which is a drink made up of sugar, salt, and water. Patients may need more than 1 gallon (3.8 l) of ORT a day for more than a week to be properly rehydrated.*

Dehydration results in a loss of essential substances that keep the body's **organs** working properly. This can cause extreme tiredness, kidney and liver failure, **seizures**, and headaches. To combat this, doctors may give the patient a solution that contains **minerals** through a drip so that the body can continue to function.

Under Control

Ebola patients may also be given medicine to reduce their vomiting and control their **blood pressure**. Pain and fever may be targeted with painkillers. If patients begin to struggle to breathe, they may be given oxygen. Sometimes patients also develop infections other than Ebola, which may need to be treated with antibiotics.

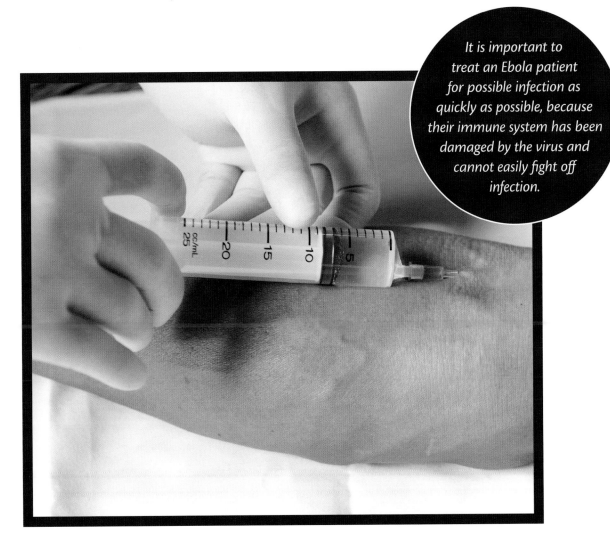

It is important to treat an Ebola patient for possible infection as quickly as possible, because their immune system has been damaged by the virus and cannot easily fight off infection.

Taking It to the Front Line

Today, scientists know that the best way to fight Ebola is to stop it spreading as soon as the disease appears. From 2014 to 2016, an Ebola outbreak in West Africa killed 11,000 people and spread to countries in Europe and to the United States. It was only thanks to immediate and swift medical and government reaction that the virus was prevented from spreading around the world.

Shutting Down the Virus

In 2014, the WHO recognized that an outbreak of Ebola was spreading rapidly throughout West Africa and alerted authorities to act quickly to stop the virus from spreading farther. Airports were closed, schools shut, public gatherings banned, and workers told to stay at home. Next, the United States sent 3,000 military personnel to West Africa to set up treatment centers where doctors could isolate patients. This swift action helped to stop the virus from spreading out of control.

In 2014, Médecins Sans Frontières sent a 60-person team to West Africa to help contain the disease. Doctors, nurses, and hygiene experts were given personal protection equipment (PPE) to protect them from the deadly virus.

Learning Lessons

The lessons learned from the 2014–2016 crisis helped shape how experts deal with Ebola today and how they battle the disease on the **front line**. When they spot the beginning of an outbreak, they deal with it immediately. A rapid response team is sent to the area where a person has been diagnosed with Ebola. The team consists of trained experts who can track down any other people who may have been infected. The team can also handle blood samples safely, communicate with the local **community** to stop panic, prevent the spread of the infection, test the samples, and record the data, or information. This "locking down" of the disease has helped save many lives in recent years.

As soon as an outbreak of Ebola is recorded, mobile, or movable, treatment units are sent to the area. These units are used for testing and treating patients.

UNDER THE MICROSCOPE

In areas where there is an outbreak, mobile laboratories at the front line can test samples quickly and safely. The labs are like huge tents that are set up near infected areas. They have different "rooms" that are used for the various stages of testing the samples. They also have advanced equipment and full protective clothing for the technicians. The labs can test samples in two to three hours instead of two to five days.

Surviving Ebola

Patients who survive Ebola often have long-term health problems that can take many months, or even years, to improve.

Life After Ebola

Ebola survivors may report ongoing symptoms, such as difficulty breathing, pains in their joints, trouble with their eyes, extreme tiredness, stomach pains, headaches, depression, and anxiety, or high levels of stress. These can make it difficult for them to go back to life as it was before they had the illness.

Fear and Suspicion

Ebola patients do not just have to battle with physical symptoms as a result of their disease. In parts of Africa, there is a lot of fear and suspicion around Ebola. People who have had the disease are often turned away by their family and friends, and they can find it difficult to get jobs or places to live. This is because it is believed that they can still pass on the infection, but this is not true. In some places, doctors give survivors a certificate so they can prove that they are not infectious.

Patients have follow-up medical visits every few months to check their ongoing physical recovery.

CASE STUDY: FROM CAREGIVER TO PATIENT

Barbara Bono was working as a nurse in Liberia when the 2014–2016 Ebola outbreak began. On the hospital wards, nurses wore basic gowns with no PPE. When Ebola patients arrived at the hospital, there was no protective clothing, no isolation areas, and no way to test patients for Ebola.

When an Ebola patient accidentally scratched Barbara's skin through her thin gown, Barbara developed the disease and was very sick for several weeks. Outside, her family **quarantined** for 21 days but was shunned by or ignored and deliberately kept away from, friends and relatives.

Barbara survived, but felt depressed for months afterward. She decided the only way to a full recovery was to get back to work. While Barbara had been sick, things had changed at the hospital. The staff had been given proper PPE and there was a system for isolating, testing, and sending patients to a treatment center. Barbara's return to a safer working life helped her recover from her depression.

Nurses who run the hospitals are often in danger of catching Ebola from sick patients if they do not have the correct protective clothing.

New Weapons

Since the first outbreak of Ebola in 1976, scientists around the world have been developing ways to fight the disease. Although there is still no cure, there are now treatments, such as vaccines, to help patients survive this terrible illness.

Medical Breakthroughs

In August 2019, doctors announced two new treatments they had been testing on Ebola patients. Both treatments involved giving the patients **antibodies** that fight the disease.

The United States National Institute of Allergy and Infectious Diseases (NIAID) developed a treatment called mAB114 by using antibodies discovered in the blood of just one patient who had survived Ebola. As soon as Ebola is diagnosed, the patient is given a dose of the antibodies. The antibodies in this treatment lock on to the Ebola virus and keep it from entering the body's cells, so the virus cannot replicate. The treatment was first tested on monkeys, and later on humans. Tests will continue until 2023, when it is hoped the treatment can be used during future Ebola outbreaks.

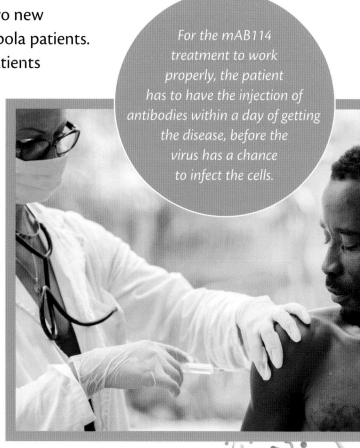

For the mAB114 treatment to work properly, the patient has to have the injection of antibodies within a day of getting the disease, before the virus has a chance to infect the cells.

Working Together

Another treatment is called ZMapp and involves a mix of three types of antibodies that were developed in a laboratory. One of the problems with targeting the Ebola virus is that it is large and changes shape, which can make it difficult for a single antibody to attack and hang on to the virus. The three antibodies work together to lock onto the virus and keep it from invading the patient's cells.

Human Trials

As with all medical research, there are many rules and regulations in place to make sure that any new drug or treatment for Ebola is thoroughly tested before it can be used. One way of testing is through **clinical trials**. For this, volunteers are used. They are given the treatment, then closely watched to see how they react. They are monitored to make sure the treatment does not have any harmful **side effects**.

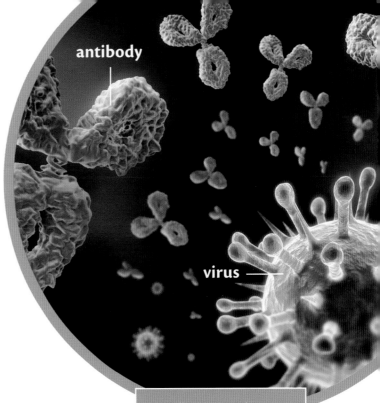

antibody

virus

This illustration shows an antibody traveling toward a virus. Once it reaches the virus, it will attack and destroy it.

UNDER THE MICROSCOPE

ZMapp was tested on patients during the 2014–2016 Ebola outbreak in Africa, but not enough people were tested to conclude that the treatment is effective enough for future use. Trials will need to continue.

Future Warfare

With every outbreak of Ebola, doctors learn more about the disease. Scientists are working on a cure, and health care workers are looking for better ways to contain the spread of infection.

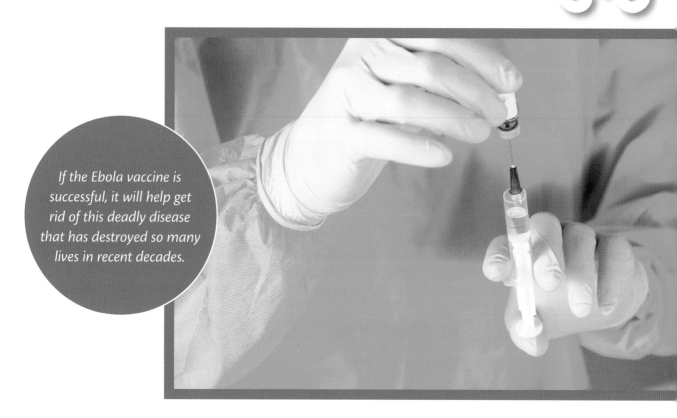

If the Ebola vaccine is successful, it will help get rid of this deadly disease that has destroyed so many lives in recent decades.

Weapons of the Future

Scientists around the world are working on vaccines that could be used to help prevent future Ebola outbreaks. A vaccine injects a tiny dose of the Ebola virus into a human cell. The cell thinks it is being attacked and produces antibodies to fight the virus. If the same person is ever infected with the Ebola virus in the future, that person will have the antibodies needed to fight off the virus.

Clinical Trials

Two vaccines have had small clinical trials in which they have been tested on volunteers to see how well they work and how safe they are. The testing has been so positive that the vaccines are now used to protect doctors and health care workers who are on the Ebola front line. However, further clinical trials are needed before either vaccine can be fully licensed for use.

Contain and Control

Until a vaccine is successful and can be used to prevent Ebola outbreaks, the only way to fight the disease is to diagnose it early and stop it from spreading. Medical authorities are working hard to train health care workers to recognize its symptoms and to isolate patients so they cannot infect others. By preventing Ebola outbreaks, the world can try to contain the disease until a cure is found.

Appelle le **115** *pour info*

EBOLA
Est une Réalité

Lavons-nous les mains au savon

unicef

There is currently a big drive to educate young people about Ebola so they have the knowledge to protect themselves and those around them. Education also helps overcome the suspicion that surrounds the disease.

"

"This vaccine is being pushed forward under emergency conditions, but we still have quite a way to go... Also, there are other vaccines in clinical trials that may complete testing...for use in the future. That is to be hoped for."

Dr. Jane Seward, Senior Advisor, Sierra Leone trials

"

Timeline

Over time, scientists have learned more about this deadly enemy and have found ways to treat and isolate cases of Ebola.

1976 The first Ebola outbreak occurs near the Ebola River in what is now the Democratic Republic of the Congo (DRC).

1989 Scientists discover the virus is passed from animals to humans.

1994 An outbreak occurs in Cote d'Ivoire in Africa.

1994 Scientists have a better understanding of how the virus is spread by touch, and by infected equipment and blood. Health care workers are given gloves, gowns, masks, and throw-away syringes.

2001 The National Microbiology Laboratory in Winnipeg, Canada, starts to research ways to treat Ebola.

2014–2016 To date, the largest and most deady Ebola outbreak occurs in Guinea, Sierra Leone, and Liberia. Reported cases total 28,616 and 11,310 people die. Health workers realize that most cases are being transmitted through burial services so safe ways to bury people are introduced.

2015 NIAID and the Ministry of Health in Liberia form the Partnership for Research on Ebola Virus in Liberia (PREVAIL). PREVAIL starts testing two possible Ebola treatments. As the outbreak in Liberia comes to an end, PREVAIL begins a large research trial to test people who have survived the virus. This reveals that chances of survival could be connected to genes.

2018 During an outbreak of Ebola in the DRC, several organizations begin clinical trials of a treatment using antibodies. The treatment increases the chances of patient survival.

2019 The United States Food and Drug Administration (FDA) approves the Ervebo® vaccine.

2019 The **European Commission** gives the Ervebo® vaccine permission to become licensed for limited use while more testing is done.

2020 Johnson & Johnson, a pharmaceutical company, is given approval from the European Commission for its vaccine. This is a two-dose vaccine: the patient has one injection when diagnosed with the illness and another eight weeks later. The company applied for an emergency-use authorization from the United States in February 2021.

Glossary

antibodies Substances produced by the body that fight off invading bacteria and viruses

bacteria Microscopic organisms that can cause infection and sickness

blood pressure The force with which blood is pumped around the body

blood vessels Tubes inside the body through which blood flows

cells The smallest units of a living thing that can survive on their own, carrying out a range of life processes

clinical trials Research performed on people to discover more about disease treatment

community A group of people living in the same place

contaminated Made dirty or infected

diagnose Confirm that a person has an illness

dispose To get rid of

electron Extremely small piece of matter with a negative electrical charge

European Commission The part of the European Union responsible for proposing laws, upholding E.U. treaties, and managing day-to-day business of the E.U.

front line An area of greatest danger

gene Instructions contained in cells that are passed down from parents to children

hemorrhagic fever An illness that causes bleeding and a high temperature

hydrated Having plenty of water

immune system The parts of the body that work together to protect it against sickness

isolating Being kept away from other people to stop a disease spreading

malaria A disease caused when a person is bitten by a disease-carrying mosquito

microscope A device that magnifies, or makes bigger, tiny objects that can otherwise not be seen with the naked eye

minerals Substances needed by the body for growth and life

organism A living thing

organs Parts of the body, such as the heart and lungs, that have specific functions

outbreaks Infection of more than one person

primates A group of animals that includes humans, apes, monkeys, and chimpanzees

quarantined Had to stay in a certain place for a certain length of time to stop the spread of infection

rehydrate To replace lost fluids

remote Far away from major cities

resources Useful supplies, such as medicine, people, or equipment

rural Not in the city or a built-up area

sample A small amount of something, such as blood, for testing

seizures Sudden uncontrolled activities in the brain that can cause mental and physical symptoms such as shaking

side effects Unpleasant effects that taking a certain drug has on a person, such as making them feel dizzy

suspicious Not trusting in something or someone

technicians Experts who work in laboratories

transmission Spreading of disease from one person to another

typhoid fever A disease spread by bacteria that results in a red rash

vaccines Substances that help protect against certain diseases

virus A microscopic organism that can cause sickness

volunteers People who offer to do something for no pay

white blood cells Cells that attack and destroy enemy invaders, such as bacteria

World Health Organization (WHO) An organization that helps governments improve their health services

Learning More

Find out more about Ebola and how the war against this deadly disease is being won.

Books

Lewis, Mark L. *Ebola: How a Viral Fever Changed History* (Infected!). Capstone Press, 2019.

Newman, Patricia. *Ebola: Fears and Facts*. Millbrook Press, 2015.

Wood, John. *Bacteria in Our World* (Under the Microscope). KidHaven Publishing, 2020.

Websites

Find out more about the Ebola virus at:
https://kids.britannica.com/students/article/Ebola/311099

Learn all about the immune system and how it helps people to stay healthy at:
https://kidshealth.org/en/kids/immune.html

Discover more about viruses, then take a quiz to test your knowledge at:
www.ducksters.com/science/biology/viruses.php

Read the amazing and inspiring true stories of people who have survived Ebola at:
www.who.int/features/2014/ebola-survivor-stories/en/

Index

ABOUT THE AUTHOR

Sarah Eason has written many science books for children, from space to biology. She particularly loves finding out how our complicated and fascinating human bodies work.